IMAGES
of London

BETHNAL
GREEN

IMAGES
of London

BETHNAL GREEN

Gary Haines

TEMPUS

George Gardens, 1903. An echo of Bethnal Green's rural past. The houses in this area in 1848 were described by contemporaries as being in a deplorable condition.

Frontispiece: Bethnal Green Library, 1960. Three women have just visited the 'By-gone Bethnal Green' exhibition and seem excited by what they have seen. One can only imagine what they would have thought if they had known that in the twenty-first century they would feature in the history of the area by their inclusion in this book!

First published 2002, reprinted 2003

Tempus Publishing Limited
The Mill, Brimscombe Port,
Stroud, Gloucestershire, GL5 2QG

© Gary Haines and London Borough of Tower Hamlets Local History Library, 2002

The right of Gary Haines and London Borough of Tower Hamlets Local History Library to be identified as the Author of this work has been asserted by them in accordance with the Copyrights, Designs and Patents Act 1988.

British Library Cataloguing in Publication Data.
A catalogue record for this book is available from the British Library.

ISBN 0 7524 2677 X

Typesetting and origination by Tempus Publishing Limited
Printed in Great Britain by Midway Colour Print, Wiltshire

Contents

This book is dedicated to Jean and Eric Haines, who are my best friends and the best Mum and Dad, thank you for everything.

Acknowledgements

My thanks go to Chris Lloyd, Local History Librarian of Tower Hamlets Local History Library and Archives, Bancroft Road, for his help, time and suggestions for this book. David Rich of Tower Hamlets Local History Library and Archives for listening to me going on about Bethnal Green again and again and for his help and support. Special thanks goes to Malcolm Barr-Hamilton, archivist at Tower Hamlets Local History Library and Archives, a good friend, for all his help, assistance and encouragement on this book, and for putting up with me as a volunteer for over four years! John Porter for being a mate through three years of university and for his support and encouragement with this project. Thanks also goes to his family; Jill, Mark and Nick. Vicky Children, Maria Stephenson and Rezia Choudhury for their encouragement from the beginning. Francesca Wolf, Jan Pollock, Anne Hartree, and all the other staff at The Fresh Horizons Department at the City Lit for giving me a future. Dr Elaine Graham-Leigh for telling me to chill out at various stages and for encouraging me to carry on my academic studies. All the staff of the History Department at Queen Mary College who knew me and helped make my three years there challenging and enjoyable. Finally to Matilda Pearce and Amy Rigg for all their hard work at Tempus Publishing, Alfred Gardner; a fellow writer with a passion for the history of the East End, and Lauren Roberts for her friendship.

Photograph Acknowledgements

I acknowledge with thanks, the following for the use of the photographs:
Tower Hamlets Local History Library and Archives, Bethnal Green Mission church, Iris Bidermans, Bishopsgate Library and Institute, The British Library, Central News Ltd, J.E. Connor, The Cooper family, William Gordon Davis, Terry Doxly, E. Edwards, Fox Photos Ltd, Halifax Photos Ltd, Edward Harris, A. Harrison, *Illustrated London News* Picture Library, Mr Jones, Jane Levy, Mr A.O. Lockwood, London Metropolitan Archives, John Maltby, Phillip Mernick, Mrs Brenda R. Prevost, L.E. Muller & Son, NCH, Mr A. Newton, Planet News Ltd, Mrs Jane Quelch, Mr A.S. Ramsey, E.D. Richardson, St James the Less church, K.G. Sheppard, Sport and General Press Agency, Mr Stanley, A.W. Tiffin, *The Times* Newspapers Ltd, Truman's Brewery, Mr W. Turner, A.E. Walsham, Walsham's Ltd, Renee Weller, William Whiffin Photograph Collection, Whitechapel Mission, Andrew Wyatt.

Introduction

A 'Happy Nook'

Bethnal Green, in the heart of London's East End, is an area famous for the legend of the blind beggar, and for having been represented as the classic example of the abundant East End slum conditions in the nineteenth century. However Bethnal Green and its history consists of much more than these. From its rural beginnings to its present-day regeneration, it is hoped that this book captures some of this journey.

The earliest reference to Bethnal Green can be found in a thirteenth-century deed, in which Mathilda le Vayre grants some of her courtyard in 'Blithehall'. The name probably derives from the Anglo-Saxon name *blithe*, meaning happy, and *haelth* meaning angle, corner or nook. It may also derive from a personal name, 'Blida'. Although there was some development in the Bethnal Green area in the Roman and Saxon periods, the first settlement of any substance was in the medieval period. This had an area of green at its centre, which in the present-day exists as Bethnal Green Gardens. In this age Bethnal Green was served by many roads which linked it with the City of London and all parts of East London.

Our small village gradually expanded, and in the sixteenth and seventeenth centuries the area became a rural retreat from the City of London, enhanced by its three mansions. The attraction of Bethnal Green for the 'well-to-do' was further added to in 1649, when an academy for gentlemen was opened by Sir Balthazar Gerbier, who at one time counted the painter Ruebens among his house guests. Evidence of rural Bethnal Green may be found in an account by Samuel Pepys of a visit he made to his friend Sir William Ryder in June 1663, who lived in Bethnal House. In his account Pepys mentions that in Ryder's garden was a great quantity of strawberries of good quality. It is in this period that the 'Ballad of the Blind Beggar of Bethnal Green' appears, and was spread by ballad singers and publishers. The legend is about the daughter of a blind beggar, probably in the fifteenth century, who had four suitors. One of these, a knight called Montford, wanted to marry the poor blind man's daughter and only discovered later that the beggar was wealthy.

After 1685 the economy and landscape altered from a pastoral one, with its few mansions and its green, to one that had to cater for its expanding population, especially of immigrants from France. Louis XIV of France revoked the Edict of Nantes, in 1685, a treaty that guaranteed freedom of worship to Protestants in the country. Many Protestants fled in fear of their lives, fearing religious persecution, and made their way to England. Some 15,000 eventually settled in London and its outskirts. This had extensive repercussions for Bethnal Green.

By 1724 Daniel Defoe, writing in his *Tour Through England and Wales*, highlighted the enormous number of buildings that had been constructed on the eastern edges of the City and the number of people now living in them. Bethnal Green had become the over-spill area for the overcrowded living and working conditions of the French Huguenot silk weavers of Spitalfields, which is to the south of Bethnal Green.

The affluent times many weavers experienced in the eighteenth and early nineteenth centuries were not to last. In 1826 when the complete ban on foreign silks, which had so far been in effect, was replaced by a custom duty, the result for independent silk weavers was more work for less pay. Often weavers and their looms would be heard in their workshops in Bethnal Green working at two or three in the morning so that they could earn enough to eat.

From the eighteenth century onwards, rural Bethnal Green became more developed. The population grew to such an extent that an Act of Parliament was passed in 1743 giving authority to create a new church, St Matthew's, for the residents. Bethnal Green now had boundaries carved from the parish boundary of St Dunstan's church, Stepney. Some three years after Bethnal Green became a separate parish it is estimated that its population was 15,000. This had risen to 45,678 by 1821 and thirty years later had reached 90,193.

The increase in the population, as the late Roy Porter described in *London: A Social History*, turned Bethnal Green from a semi-rural area into a parish that could reasonably be described as London's poorest. This increase brought an even greater demand for housing. No public transport meant that you had to live near your place of work. An examination of the trade directory entry for Bethnal Green Road in 1888 reveals the diversity of employment. Along this road one could find among other trades, sixteen butchers, ten bakers, ten public houses, eight surgeons and six tailors, alongside ten boot and shoemakers, three cabinet makers, a cotton yarn manufacturer, two dairies, a rope-maker and a saddler.

The demand for more housing meant more overcrowding and worsening sanitary conditions, and by the middle of the nineteenth century Bethnal Green was notorious as an appalling slum. Cholera would visit this area four times in the nineteenth century. Attempts were made by organizations and individuals both inside and outside the parish to rectify these problems. One of these attempts was the large-scale clearance undertaken in the Boundary Street area by the London County Council in 1891, as St Matthews vestry could not develop the area.

The London Government Act of 1899 replaced old vestries and district boards with twenty-eight boroughs, and so Bethnal Green become a Metropolitan Borough in 1900, with its boundaries virtually unchanged. In the 1920s and '30s slum clearances were undertaken by the borough and London County Council. The events of the Second World War also gave an opportunity to rebuild on the bombsites. One of the biggest post-war building schemes was the Cranbrook Estate, built in the late 1950s. In 1965 Bethnal Green was integrated into the London Borough of Tower Hamlets, along with the Stepney and Poplar Metropolitan Boroughs.

The post-war period, which saw Bethnal Green assume the appearance it has today, brought depopulation. The densely populated Bethnal Green of the nineteenth century was to lose its people through migration to towns, in counties such as Essex, and to new estates outside Bethnal Green, whose tenants were encouraged to move there by the London County Council. The shift in population is one of the most striking aspects of the history of Bethnal Green in the twentieth century. In 1901 the population had been some 130,000, however this had more then halved to 47,330 by 1941. By 1981 30,000 people lived in Bethnal Green. The population of Bethnal Green has seen many cultures, from the Huguenots and the Jews through to the present-day Black and Asian communities. Each has added something to the unique blend of history that is Bethnal Green. In recent years Bethnal Green has again become a much sought-after place to live. The regeneration of the area has seen property prices rise dramatically.

The chapters in this book have been designed to reflect the main themes of the history of Bethnal Green, its people and its buildings. It is hoped that this book and its photographs, in its own small way, serves as a tribute to the 'Bethnal Greener's' of the past, the present and the future.

One

Housing in
Bethnal Green

Lamb Gardens, c. 1870. Much of the origin of the place name 'Garden' can be seen in this photograph. The cottages were occupied by weavers. Lamb Garden's, Place and Row consisted of narrow lanes and converted garden sheds turned into dwellings.

Mary and John Sheppard at their house, No. 63 Orange Street, off Gossett Street, July 1903. They were married at St Matthew's parish church on 31 December 1888 and had four children, Mary, George Phillip, Margaret and Willie, known as Andrew, who can be seen sitting next to his mum. Mary Sheppard died in December 1904, and her husband in January 1922. Orange Street became part of Satchwell Road in July 1937.

George Gardens, 1903. This name originates from the gardens that were present at one time in the vicinity of the 'Old George' pub, which can be seen in the background. Due to the upsurge in population in the area, garden sheds would at times be converted into dwellings.

Pettits Walk, in the 1860s. This view looks towards Waterlow Buildings in Wilmot Street, which had recently been built by the Improved Industrial Dwellings Company Ltd. The buildings in the foreground, which are remarkably rural in appearance, were soon to be replaced by similar model dwellings. In this clearance scheme three new streets were created; Corfield, Ainsley and Finnis.

Cranbrook Street, early twentieth century. It was estimated that in 1914, 114 weavers occupied forty-six workshops in Cranbrook Street and Alma Road. It has been suggested that the name Cranbrook derives from the village in Kent, where in 1331 Edward III established looms to foster the English weaving industry and so prevent the Flemish from profiting by processing the English raw wool.

Merceron Houses, Globe Road, c. 1903. In the foreground are weaver's cottages; they were demolished in 1906. Merceron Houses were built by the East End Dwellings Company founded in 1884 with the aim to house the very poor and make some profit while doing this. Merceron Houses stood out with their red and yellow bricks and were designed by Ernest Emmanuel. They were built by 1901, but were replaced in 1949 after bomb damage.

Cranbrook Street, looking east, 1933. Building began in this area in 1851 and, along with Alma Road, was a focus of the weaving industry. A Ragged school was opened at No. 39 Cranbrook Street in 1870, but was soon closed when the premises were deemed unsuitable. The large building in the distance is the Cranbrook Road London County Council school for boys, girls and infants, which opened in 1881. In 1956 the primary school was closed and the secondary school was merged with Bow school to form Bowbrook Secondary school.

A row of weaver's houses with their typically large first floor windows, Menotti Street, 1927. This street had been called Manchester Street up until 1864. The majority of Menotti Street was cleared in the 1950s to make way for Weaver's Fields, and a tiny part of the street still remains.

The rear of Nos 7-12 Butler Street, 1936. A rear view of these back-to-back houses with the interiors of the gardens being put to various uses. This street, south of Roman Road, was probably named after Richard Butler, an owner of the manor of Stepney in the

seventeenth century. A deed of 1830 gives the earliest reference to Butler Street. The street was redeveloped in the 1950s and is now situated within Butler Estate.

Weaver's houses, Derbyshire Street, 1954. These houses were built with large windows on the first flooor in order to give workshops maximum advantage from natural light.

Neath Place, 1915. Neath Place was situated east of Brady Street. In the background can be seen the covered entrance to Collingwood Street which replaced Trafalgar Place and Cumberland Place in 1884. In the 1940s the seven acre Collingwood Estate took its place.

Tent Street in the 1930s. This area was scheduled to be cleared in 1937, displacing some 505 people who were living in eighty houses. Tent Street was situated on ground originally used for drying fabric on frames by cloth manufacturers, and the name of the street gave tenants a link to this past.

Cooper's Gardens, Victoria Street, west of Gascoigne Place, c. 1915. This was probably named after Thomas Cooper, an occupier in 1779 of two acres of land between Castle Street and Hackney Road. Unhealthy conditions existed in Cooper's Gardens in 1937 when it housed 424 people in ninety-nine houses in just over two acres. Bethnal Green had six other slum clearance areas. Dunmore Point and Mildmay Mission Hospital now occupy where Cooper's Gardens once stood.

Columbia Square, 1958. Charles Dickens' suggestion to Baroness Angela Burdett-Coutts, who had inherited a fortune in 1837 and wished to use it to improve the conditions of the underprivileged to improve a part of the East End, resulted in Columbia Square. The flats were demolished in 1962 and Sivill House was built on the site.

Some tenants of Columbia Square, *c.* 1921. This group largely consists of the children resident in Columbia Square. This Square was named after the bishopric of British Columbia founded by Baroness Burdett-Coutts. Columbia Square was built on the site of Nova Scotia Gardens, an area which, arguably, was the inspiration for the 'dust heap' in Dickens' *Our Mutual Friend*. The first of the four five-storey blocks was completed in 1859 and the last in 1862. The top storey of these blocks housed reading rooms and washing/laundry facilities. More than 1,000 people moved into the new homes.

Collingwood Street, 1915. Back of houses at the junction of Collingwood and Somerfield Streets. The first post-First World War London County Council housing, Collingwood Estate, was built here between Brady and Collingwood Streets. By the end of 1927, four blocks comprising 185 flats and re-housing 1,126 people had been built.

Hereford Street, looking west from Sale Street towards Hereford Street, early twentieth century. In this street No. 61 was used as one of the George Crump Almshouses from 1933-1966. The northern part of Hereford Street, which extended past Sale Street, was cleared in the 1950s to make way for Sarel House. The spire in the background is that of St Matthew's church.

Boarded-up houses in Hollybush Gardens, *c.* 1934. Hollybush Gardens became notorious in 1863 when an investigation into the deaths of twelve children in the area revealed that 219 of the 222 houses in the area relied on a static tank and a defective pump for water. This street was cleared in 1934, displacing 115 people who were living in eighteen houses.

Pritchards Road, north of Hackney Road corner of Spencer passage, looking north, *c.* 1915. Two figures in a street that is soon to be cleared and disappear forever. The advertising boards on No. 3 Pritchards Road advertise goods bought by the locals over the years. Near the doorway of No. 1 and to the left of No. 3 is a boot scraper, which would have been used by those entering the house to clear dirt off their shoes. To the far right of the picture can be seen the large impressive building which was the King's Arms public house.

21

Ann's Place, Peace Terrace, looking towards Waterloo Terrace, in the 1930s. Ann's Place was in existence by 1819. In 1848 it was the centre of an outbreak of disease – a death in a house from cholera in Ann's Place was attributed to a dunghill and muck along the canal banks. Ann's Place was a row of houses in Pritchard's Road, which merged with Pritchard's Road in 1883. Pritchard's Road, along with the nearby Ada Place, were designated for clearance in 1934, displacing some 368 people who had been living in sixty-one houses.

Terraced Houses, Nos 326-362 Old Ford Road, September 1954, overlooking Victoria Park. These were included in Bethnal Green Borough Council's Old Ford Road clearance scheme along with Nos 304-362 (even),º Old Ford Road and No. 222 Grove Road.

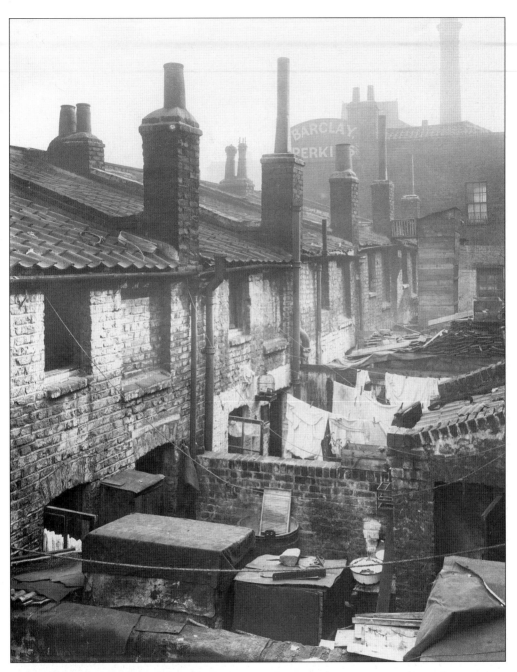

The rear of Pereira Street looking south from No. 9 Holmes Avenue, c. 1900. This area was cleared soon after the First World War. This photograph incorporates within it a lot that was indicative of living in Bethnal Green. In the foreground can be seen a washboard and a tin bath, and on the far right an outside toilet. When examining the other gardens, birdcages can be seen. The furthest garden has a large pigeon loft. The sign in the background for the brewers Barclay Perkins was on the Freemasons Arms public house. This pub was demolished during the re-developments. The large chimney, which can just be glimpsed in the distance, belonged to the Albion Brewery of Cross, Mann and Paulin on the Whitechapel Road.

Off Boundary Street, 1890. This unnamed street, which lay off Boundary Street, shows that it suffered similar conditions to those to be found in the area that it bordered, the 'Nichol'. Poor living and sanitation conditions were mentioned in Arthur Morrison's novel *A Child of the Jago*, published in 1896. In 1890 the Nichol was declared a slum, and the Boundary Street Scheme designed by Owen Fleming, was implemented. Demolition began in 1891. This large clearance scheme, undertaken by the London County Council, cleared five acres of land.

Construction of the Digby Estate, Digby Street, c. 1936. The foundation stone was laid in 1935. The Digby Estate, east of Globe Road, consisted of a five-storey brick building with fifty-five flats, and was opened in 1936. The street was named after the nineteenth-century local builder Charles Digby, who built as many houses as possible into a small area. This led to the conditions so graphically described by Dr Hector Gavin in *Sanitary Ramblings*, his published survey of sanitary conditions in 1848. He described Digby Street before clearance as being a 'whole area filled with every variety of manure in every stage of offensive and disgusting decomposition.' The new flats were comprised of thirty-three two bedroom flats and twenty-two three bedroom flats. The total cost of the construction of this estate was £29,000. A hero of the First World War is commemorated in the form of Godley House. Private Sidney Frank Godley was awarded a Victoria Cross for gallantry in Belgium defending a railway bridge near Nimy, 23 August 1914. A plaque also commemorates Private Sidney Frank Godley VC, who was a caretaker at Cranbrook school.

Opposite, below: Arnold Circus, Boundary Street Estate, 1910; the new face of the 'Nichol'. This view shows the centre of Boundary Street Estate. The roads that lead off this; Hocker, Falissy, Rochelle, Ainsworth, Camlet, Navarre and Calvert Avenue recall Huguenot associations. Twenty-three blocks were built and named after places along the Thames. The estate included a laundry, 188 shops and seventy-seven workshops. The existing churches and schools that were on the site before clearance were also there. However, twelve pubs disappeared, as this was to be a 'dry' estate. Building began in 1893 and the Prince of Wales opened the estate in 1900. The tenants that moved into this estate were largely not the original ones who had left the 'Nichol,' as they could not afford the high rents. The previous tenants moved into older property nearby and suffered overcrowding again.

Laying of commemoration stone, Greenways Estate, 1949. Although building was started on this estate in 1949, it was not finished until 1959. An extension to the estate, Jowitt House, was built on the site of St Simon Zelotes church, which was destroyed during bombing in the Second World War. The completed estate contained some 515 flats.

Laying of the foundation stone, Bethnal Green Estate, 1922. This was the Metropolitan Borough of Bethnal Green's first estate. This estate was situated at the centre of the borough. It was built on the site of Kirby Castle, otherwise known as Bethnal House, which became a private lunatic asylum in the nineteenth century. Between 1922-1924 seven four-storey blocks were built which were named after poets. In keeping with this tradition an additional block, added to the estate in 1966, was called Keats House.

Unveiling the commemoration stone, Diss Street Housing Scheme, October 1922. The housing scheme consisted of two blocks built on the site of Smith's Buildings and Smith's Place. It was known as the Vaughan Estate in honour of the mayor of Bethnal Green, Joseph Vaughan, seen here on the left of the stone. It appears that the youngsters of the area were keen to appear in this photograph.

Laying the commemoration stone, Cambridge Heath Estate, September 1926. Mayor Alderman Charles William Hovell is laying the stone. This estate is on the corner of Cambridge Heath Road and Parmiter Street and was originally known as Parmiter Street re-housing scheme. This was the Metropolitan Borough of Bethnal Green's second housing estate. The estate was controversially named 'Lenin Estate' in July 1927 by the Communist-Socialist council, and renamed 'Cambridge Heath Estate' in December 1928 by the then Liberal-progressive council. The estate was seen at the time as being lavish as it offered free electric light. The estate consisted of thirty-two flats in a four-storey block and was designed by E.C.P. Monson, the borough architect.

George Belt House, Greenways Estate, Moss Street, September 1951. The first tenant was Mrs Ellen Garner who moved into No. 2 George Belt House after living nearby for thirty-four years. She is seen here shaking hands with G.A. Stocks, acting chairman of the housing committee. The new flats had been ready since February, but a Bethnal Green electrician's strike stopped the completion of the job. The striking electricians, many of whom can be seen here (who included Councillor A. Stocks among their number) agreed to do the work without pay so they did not break the conditions of the strike, and the remaining wiring was completed in two days. The house was named after George Belt, who was a London County Council member for Bethnal Green between 1925 and 1928.

Children line up for their photograph outside Lisbon Street buildings, off Cambridge Heath Road, c. 1915. These privately-built model dwellings date from 1887. These buildings were cleared by 1939, and the site now forms part of Sainsbury's superstore.

Leopold Buildings, Columbia Road, in the 1960s. The Improved Industrial Dwellings Company built five blocks on the south side of Crabtree Row, which later became Columbia Road in 1872. These blocks accommodated 112 families. In 1965 Tower Hamlets Council acquired Leopold Buildings, which have since been extensively refurbished.

Cyprus Street looking towards Cranbrook Estate, 1972. In the foreground to the right can be seen the Duke of Wellington Public House at No. 52 Cyprus Street. By 1870 some thirty-one public houses in Bethnal Green were licensed for music and dancing, and one of these was the Duke of Wellington. The pub may have taken its name from Cyprus Street's former name, until 1879, of Wellington Street.

William Fenn House, Shipton Street, c. 1955. William Fenn House comprised of sixteen flats and maisonettes and was erected by Bethnal Green Council. It was opened in 1955 and named after William Fenn, a Bethnal Green councillor who served on the housing committee before his death in around 1952.

Mayfield House, Cambridge Heath Road, 1964. This six-storey building of white Portland stone, which incorporated the borough's music library, was opened on the 26 September 1964. It was built on the site of the Odeon Cinema, which closed in 1956. On the top floor was located six two-bedroom flats and on the other floors forty-eight one-bedroom flats. The occupiers of these flats, designed mainly for the elderly, had easy access to the public laundry on the ground floor, which would replace the one in nearby York Hall. The music library moved from its temporary home at the central library and held some 2,500 books and 4,000 records. To accompany this music library was a recital hall, which had a grand piano and a record player, and could seat seventy-seven people.

Cranbrook Estate, Roman Road looking north, c. 1969. This estate was built in 1959 on fourteen acres of cleared ground between Old Ford Road and Bonner Road by Bethnal Green Borough Council. During this clearance, terraced houses, workshops and J.J. Lanes' Phoenix Works, a large engineering firm, were all demolished. The estate was called Cranbrook, after Cranbrook Street that ran through the area. The first blocks opened in 1963 and the estate was officially opened in 1964. The estate won an award from the civic trust. As part of the building scheme, the council erected a market square off Roman Road in 1959 to stop market stalls choking up the streets. The statue in the foreground commemorates the legend of the Blind Beggar of Bethnal Green and was designed by Elizabeth Frank. Situated within the estate, the statue was unveiled in 1959.

Lakeview Estate, c. 1960. This estate is situated between Old Ford Road and the Hertford Union Canal and was built on land devastated by bombing. Only one house was left standing in this area. Lakeview Estate, which overlooks Victoria Park Lake, consists of an eleven-storey twin-tower block with two two-storey blocks, and was opened in 1958.

Sulkin House, Greenways Estate, 1961. Built as part of the second stage of the building scheme for Greenways Estate, which began in 1952, this eight-storey building with its eye-catching central column was designed by Sir Denys Lasdun, whose idea it was to create a 'vertical' street.

Two

The Streets

Houses in Old Bethnal Green Road, 1937. Old Bethnal Green Road became 'Old' when Bethnal Green Road was built to the south of it. An Act of Parliament of 1756 gave authorization to build it, which was over the line of a bridleway. Old Bethnal Green Road has a somewhat colourful past if its previous names are anything to go by; in 1642 it had been known as Rogue Lane, and as Whore's Lane in 1717.

Coate's farm and the Old George Inn, 1773. Coate's Farm occupied an area of land bounded by Pollard Row, Cambridge Heath Road and Old Bethnal Green Road. This farm, probably named after its original owners, was typical of farms to be found in the area. In the sixteenth and seventeenth centuries farming in the area consisted of a mix of arable and livestock farming, it was from the early seventeenth century that keeping cows became the most popular type of farming in the area – the main market for their milk supply would have been London. Farming would continue in the area even in the highly urbanized Bethnal Green of the middle nineteenth century. In around 1850, thirty cowmen or dairymen were in existence in the parish. By this time the market for milk was more local. In 1874 there were 408 cows and heifers in the parish adding, no doubt, to the sanitary problems of the area. The Old George, on the left of this watercolour by an unknown artist, and distinguishable by its overhanging pub sign, was still going strong in the twentieth century.

Bethnal Green Road, looking eastwards from Brick Lane, 1905. Street traders sell flowers, and C. Page & Co., on the left of the picture, were cane dealers. This western section of Bethnal Green Road was called Church Street until 1879. Church Street was found to be in need of widening because it was the main thoroughfare from the developing Victoria Park district to the City and Finsbury. The Metropolitan Board of Works obtained an Act of Parliament in 1872 to enable them to widen the road and at the same time clear slums in the area. In 1879 the new road, called Bethnal Green Road throughout, was opened.

Opposite, below: The west side of Cambridge Road, now Cambridge Heath Road, in the 1920s. In 1919 you could buy a newspaper at No. 1 Cambridge Road, where H. Phillips was news vendor, then choose between No. 3 The Cambridge Coffee and Dining Rooms or No. 5 Robert Cooke's Eel and Pie Shop, for refreshments while you read. One can see tramlines embedded into the road. These were put in by the North Metropolitan Lines Company, who ran red trams along this road in 1893, calling it the 'Museum Line,' because it took passengers to Bethnal Green Museum situated on this road.

Public transport going 'Up West' on Bethnal Green Road, looking eastwards, *c.* 1903. On the left of the picture can be seen St James the Great church, otherwise known as the 'Red church', which was assigned in 1844. Its vicar from 1852-97 was Edward Fraser Coke, a somewhat controversial figure among his church companions. Coke highlighted the needs of the poor in the area and helped to raise money for them by advertising in *The Times* newspaper. He also helped to found Queen Adelaide dispensary, and, perhaps most controversially, offered to conduct marriages for a seven-penny fee. This resulted in somewhat animated scenes around the church and in many young couples getting married in groups. The church was called the 'Red church' due to its red brick construction, the first in the East End. The parsonage was united with St Jude's in 1954, and with St Matthew's in 1984. St James' has now been converted into flats. Bethnal Green Road appears on Gascoyne's map of 1703 and can arguably be traced back to Roman times. The improvements made by the Metropolitan Board of Works, which took place in 1879, gave it its present shape – these improvements include the building of a new section from Brick Lane to Shoreditch High Street.

Opposite: Roman Road, looking east, *c.* 1906. 'The Roman', as it is known locally, is busy with traffic. It is possible that this road was used in Roman times to enable travel from London to Essex however, with the end of Roman occupation, this road fell into disuse. The road was then rebuilt and called Green Street and Roman Road. The stretch of Roman Road that is in Bethnal Green (the rest being in Bow) was not called Roman Road until 1938, when it changed from Green Street. The church on the left of the picture is St Barnabas.

Dixie Street, seen from Brady Street, *c.* 1900. This street was cleared by 1948 and replaced with Codrington House. The pub on the corner of Dixie Street, the Duke of Wellington, survived the widening of the road which changed its address to Scott Street.

Junction of Brady Street and Merceron Street, *c.* 1908. Children walk past No. 82 Brady Street, which was owned by Herbert Edwards Holmes, a pawnbroker. The shop to the left of this, at No. 84, was called The Vienna; a laundry business run by Israel Schneider in 1908.

Numbers 74-76 Cheshire Street, 1953. This portion of Cheshire Street was known as Hare Street until 1938. Nathan Lazarus at No. 76 Hare Street was a watch repairer and No. 74 was a plywood merchant. The large windows above these shops show that these premises were occupied by weavers at one time. In 1953 one can see that a horse and cart was still used in Bethnal Green for deliveries.

Neath Place, northern side, looking west from Tapp Street junction in the early twentieth century. Children play in the streets, amusing themselves. Two boys seem particularly fascinated by something they have found on the road.

Pelter Street, off Diss Street, *c.* 1920. There is a family likeness in the faces of the group that pose for the camera, which may mean they are three generations of the same family. One little girl seems to have become shy and is hiding. Pelter Street was known as Willow Walk until 1905 and was renamed Pelter Street after a sixteenth-century landowner. These houses were cleared when Vaughan Estate was constructed, and Pelter Street was extended in the late 1960s.

Opposite, below: Old Ford Road, photographed from the south west, December 1960. The shops at Numbers 53-59 Old Ford Road were demolished. The newly-built housing visible behind these shops was named James Campbell House, in commemoration of the General Secretary of the National Union of Railwaymen. James Campbell was killed in a motoring accident while on an official visit to the USSR in November 1957, along with the President of the National Union of Railwaymen Tom Hollywood. James Campbell House was opened in 1963.

A baker's shop at No. 130 Brady Street, December 1915. This photograph produces evidence of the effect of the First World War on businesses in the area. In 1911 this shop was W. Watson's, a butchers shop. By 1915 the shop, still occupied by W. Watson, became a baker's. Government food regulations during the war caused many traders to change their businesses, for example restrictions placed on meat meant that a better living could be made from baking instead. The wall butress at No. 130 was erected by the London County Council due to dangerous defective brickwork.

Eastman Street, south side, at the junction with Brady Street, September 1960. This area was included in Bethnal Green Eastman Street compulsory purchase order of 1958 for clearance. King's Laundries Ltd is on the corner at No. 45, which in the past had been, variously, a butcher's in 1930 and a chandler's shop in 1911.

Cambridge Heath Road, west side, viewed from No. 161 looking south, 1950. The Carpenters Arms public house is in the centre of the houses at No. 151. This pub can be traced at this address from at least 1837.

Preston Street, looking north towards Roman Road, May 1951. The area was cleared and became the site of George Belt House, part of the Greenways Estate. The large building in the distance is Cranbrook Primary and Secondary schools.

Cambridge Heath Road, 31 January 1961, looking northwards. Going past St John's church is a No. 653 trolleybus on its last day of service. The next day it was replaced with the new 253 bus route. The London County Council ran electric trams along this route from 1910. An Empress Omnibus garage was built in Corbridge Crescent, just off Cambridge Heath Road, in 1925. The London Passenger Transport Board introduced trolleybuses along Cambridge Heath Road in 1939, but in 1958 motorbuses were run along this route instead.

Numbers 70-86 Seabright Street, south of Bethnal Green Road, 1953. The large windows of these houses echo back to the former occupants who were weavers and needed a lot of light to work by. By 1836 there were 1,976 houses south of Bethnal Green Road, many of which, like these houses in Seabright Street, would have been occupied by weavers.

Street improvement, Teale Street, looking westwards to Goldsmiths Row, c. 1940. Teale Street was named after its builder, Joseph Teale, of Shoreditch, who had constructed it by 1836.

Cheshire Street, looking east, June 1926, showing road improvements being undertaken. The large building in the background on the left is the Cheshire Street Baths, situated on the corner with Abbey Street. These baths and washhouses were opened in 1899, and were the first in Bethnal Green to be built under the Baths and Washhouses Act. The western section was occupied by a public laundry, an ironing and mangling room and a women's bathing area. This part closed in 1974 and was then occupied by Repton Boy's Club and used as a boxing club and gym. Repton's boxers often represent the country at Olympic level. The eastern section housed the main men's baths and these closed in 1978. In 1990 planning permission was given to develop a leisure club on this section and in 1994 it was to be partially converted into flats.

Roman Road, 1961. Looking west from near No. 285. On Gascoyne's map of 1703 the western portion of Roman Road was marked as Driftway. The road is not marked in its entirety until the 1740s. It was called Green Street by 1790, and is still referred to as such by some locals. The road here was widened in 1887 and again in the 1960s.

Roman Road, August 1952, showing Numbers 180-200 (even), prior to their clearance. On the far right at No. 180 is the Angel and Crown public house. The drapers at No. 194 has an 1897 date stone, but when it first appears in the trade directory for 1897 it is listed as a fried fish shop.

Sclater Street, c. 1965. This deserted street was the site of the pet market until it closed in 1983 and which spilt over from Club Row. The street's name is connected with land owned by Thomas Sclater. The area was known as Slaughter's Land in 1703 and Slaughter's Street 1799. This street has an interesting history; a complaint by a rector against the Sun alehouse in the street in 1816 was due to men and women meeting in a 'cock and hen club' where they 'get drunk and debauch each other'.

Cambridge Heath Road, 1950s, looking east towards Old Ford Road. The site of Mayfield House is to the left and Bethnal Green Museum is to the right. The road sign crossed out is the Cambridge Road sign. Cambridge Road became Cambridge Heath Road in 1938. Mayfield House was constructed on a narrow site, once the site of the old Mayfield House, which in 1919 housed a temporary library and Dr Bates' surgery. The new Mayfield House opened in 1964.

Three
Education and Welfare

Gifts being distributed at Bethnal Green Town Hall, 1949. Four hundred local children visited the Town Hall on 24 February 1949 to receive gift parcels from Canada. These parcels are distributed here by the mayor, councillor G.R.H. Hemsley JP, and members of the Women's Voluntary Services. The parcels contained – much to the children's delight – salmon, spam, peaches, drinking chocolate, biscuits, sweets, chewing gum, eating chocolate and a book. All of these would have been gratefully received in an era of post-war austerity and rationing.

The Watch House, St Matthew's churchyard, Wood Street, c. 1890. Bethnal Green had a watch house by 1652 and was marked on a map in the centre of the Driftway and Bethnal Green Road. In 1676 Bethnal Green Hamlet was ordered to pay the constable for a 'very needful' stocks and whipping post which he had purchased. A new watch house was built in 1754 in the churchyard of St Matthew's to curb body snatching. Burials at the new church had begun in 1746. In 1826, the year the watch house pictured here was built, the 'Bullock Hunters', a gang 500-600 strong, met every night in Bethnal Green to rob shops of food and ambush animals going to Smithfield and Barnet markets. Sir Robert Peel, the Home Secretary, in reaction to this outbreak, stationed forty men in the parish and sent out horse patrols in an attempt to re-establish law and order. The subsequent arrests deterred the gang. A police station was established at 458 Bethnal Green Road in 1869 and remained here until 1995 when it and Leman Street police station moved into new premises in Victoria Park Square.

Opposite, below: Class 1 of Bonner Street Infants school, c. 1883. Bonner Street school was opened by the School Board for London in 1876, built in the mock Queen Anne style on the site of Twig Folly British Girl's school. It was remodelled in 1914-15. This school was renamed Bonner Primary in 1949 and it was where the author became a pupil and first developed his interest in history! Bonner Street and Bonner Road were named after Bishop Edmund Bonner, Bishop of London in the mid-sixteenth century. He was a Catholic Bishop, deposed in 1549, who sought retribution in the reign of Mary Tudor when he was restored, persecuting many Protestants. In 1559 he refused to take the Oath of Supremacy which would make Elizabeth I the head of the Church of England, and for this he was again deposed and imprisoned in Marshalsea where he died in 1569. He was buried at the church of St George the Martyr in Southwark.

Pupils of Morpeth school in their classroom with their teacher, in the 1920s. The expressions of the children vary from happiness to boredom, much like the expressions to be found in classrooms today! This school was opened in 1910 as Morpeth Street Central school. After the Second World War it became a mixed senior school with general, technical and commercial courses, in new premises linked to the old premises, including the buildings of Portman Place school. In 1974 a block containing workshops, gym, library and a hall was added. Morpeth Street school has recently been further renovated.

The whole community at the National Children's Home in Bonner Road, 1871. The orphanage was originally based in Stockwell in South London until it moved to premises in Bonner Road, next to Victoria Park church, in 1871. Thomas Bowman Stephenson, minister of Victoria Park Baptist church, was appointed to the home in 1873. Larger premises were built in Bonner Road in 1877. The children's home moved in 1913 to a new orphanage in Harpenden, near St Albans. Victoria Park church, which it had been linked with, declined and closed in 1928. It reopened as the Bethnal Green Central Hall in 1929, as the 'Church of the Happy Welcome'. The orphanage is now located in Highbury, north London, where it moved in 1925.

Opposite, below: Bethnal Green Medical Mission, Cambridge Heath Road, 29 September 1955. A London County Council ambulance is outside the Medical Mission. The first medical mission was situated at No. 60 Commercial Street in an old warehouse used for victims of the Cholera epidemic of 1866. In 1867 under the direction of Annie Macpherson, whose aim was to improve conditions among matchmakers, No. 29 Bethnal Green Road was opened. These premises were known as the 'Home of Industry'. Medical work began in 1901. Miss Macpherson's nephew, Mr Merry, was the first doctor. Within the first eight months, 2,700 patients had visited the dispensary doctor and nurses. Some 1,000 visits were made to homes. This saw a new emphasis on medical work and in November 1925 premises at 305 Cambridge Heath Road were opened. A year later the name was changed to The Bethnal Green Medical Mission with the added name in brackets 'The Annie Macpherson Home of Industry Inc.' The building was extensively rebuilt, culminating in a brand new building being opened in 1955. The surgery of the Medical Mission recently moved to newly built premises in Cambridge Heath Road on the site of the former Bethnal Green Hospital and was renamed The Mission practise.

National Children's Home, 1870s. Three occupants, possibly from the same family, photographed to publicise the work of the National Children's Home. In advertising for the home on the occasion of its new premises opening in Bonner Road, it was stated that the Home was 'for the rescue of children who, through the death or vice or extreme poverty of their parents, are in danger of falling into criminal ways'.

Bethnal Green Medical Mission Sunday school meeting, c. 1950. In 1945 the Sunday school was at the height of its popularity, providing two teenage Bible classes, sixteen junior Sunday school groups and two infant groups, all in operation at the same time. For these classes, thirty-three teachers were needed. A small bookshop situated in the Medical Mission also sold religious education books, and the small display window of this shop was a gift of the Clarendon school.

Bethnal Green Infirmary, 1904. The Bethnal Green Poor Law Guardians bought the site of the Episcopal Jew's Chapel and associated buildings in 1895. Their aim was to build an infirmary for the sick of Bethnal Green Workhouse. The three-storey red brick building opened in 1900 and had a central administration block and three double-ward blocks to the west of this. In 1901 it is recorded that the infirmary was occupied by 619 inmates and 117 officials. Part of the infirmary building survives today as luxury flats in Cambridge Heath Road.

Bethnal Green Infirmary, nurses relaxing in their recreation room, c. 1910. In 1926 receiving wards were built and a central block added in 1927, an operating theatre was installed in 1929. The infirmary was bombed during the war. 1950 saw the infirmary reclassified as a general or acute hospital. Between 1978-1985 the hospital was reclassified again as a geriatric hospital and, in this time span, bed numbers were reduced. The hospital finally closed in 1988 and was partially demolished.

St James the Less Working Men's Hotel, Ames Street, early twentieth century. This hotel was converted from three houses in Ames Street, Nos 2, 4 and 6, after previously being situated in No. 6 only. It was stated that the Working Men's Hotel had sleeping facilities for seventy-five men of the 'coster' type. This hotel, or hostel as it was latterly termed, was still in operation during the period of the Second World War when it was running at a loss due to lack of men using the facilities. This was by no means the only facility run by St James the Less – on the opening of the new parochial buildings in 1901, the church ran, among other things, day schools, workshops, a reading room, a dispensary and a gym.

Victoria Park Chest Hospital, 1916, later known as the London Chest Hospital. Beds were put on the veranda, so that the patients could breathe fresher air. In 1849 a committee of largely Quaker businessmen rented four acres of land near the recently built Victoria Park. Bishop's Hall and its buildings were demolished for the building of the hospital. Prince Albert laid the foundation stone of the hospital in 1851 and it opened as a consumption hospital in 1855. 1858 saw the building of a chapel and other rebuilding and enlargements took place in 1881, 1891 and 1899. The hospital was renamed the City of London Hospital for Diseases of the Heart and Lungs in 1923 and in 1928 a surgical block and X-ray department was added. The hospital was damaged by bombing during the war, destroying the chapel and a hospital wing. Further extensions to the building have been added in the 1970s and '80s.

Opposite: Bethnal Green Memorial Hall and Bethnal Green Free Library, London Street, (later called Dunbridge Street), 1903. The Memorial Hall was erected in 1875. The Free Library was founded by the Christian community in 1875, and from cramped quarters in London Street the library moved in 1881 to the Memorial Hall. Funds and books for the library came from many famous people of the time, including King Edward VII and Queen Victoria, and by 1882 the library had over 7,000 volumes. The library unsuccessfully applied to move to a site on the Poor's Land in 1888. The library closed in 1934 due to the opening of public libraries in October 1922, which were able to attract readers who wanted a wider range of books than the Free Library could provide.

Bethnal Green Town Hall, Patriot Square, 1939. The previous Town Hall was situated in Church Row. In 1908 the council acquired the site on the corner of Cambridge Road and Patriot Square and the new Town Hall was opened in 1910. The picture shows the new extension on the left, which was built between 1936-39, and the older building on the extreme right.

Rear entrance of Bethnal Green Library, 1960. Mr William Crook pictured with a bicycle and a stack of books. Books would be distributed around the borough by truck or, in this case, by bicycle to branch libraries. In 1980 Mr Crook's wife Lillian was elected mayor of Bethnal Green. Both were life-long 'Bethnal Greeners'. Mr Crooks worked for thirty-five years as a library porter, retiring in 1970, and was well known as a calligrapher producing beautifully inscribed pieces on many subjects, but particularly local history and Shakespeare. Mr and Mrs Crook were residents of William Fenn House.

The adult section of Bethnal Green Library, *c. 1922*. The site of the library dates back to the 1500s and has a history that would in itself fill the shelves of the adult library viewed here. In 1570 Bethnal House was constructed for John Kirby on this site. By 1660 the house had been purchased by William Ryder, and it was here that Pepys visited and brought his diaries for safety during the Great Fire of London. From 1727 this site, under a lease to Matthew Wright, was used as a lunatic asylum and this was its use for the next 200 years. In 1843 Bethnal House was demolished and rebuilt, and in 1896 more rebuilding added a male inmates block to this site. In 1921 Bethnal House was purchased by the local council and the property was adapted for a library at a cost of £36,000, opening in 1922, with an extension designed by A.E. Darby. The library contained an adult lending library, a children's library, a lecture hall and a newsroom. The stock numbered some 50,000 volumes, and by 1924 over one million books had been issued. The intense history of this site is reflected in the local name given to the grounds surrounding the library by the locals, 'Barmy Park'.

Newspaper and magazine reading room of Bethnal Green Library, c. 1922. This library would stock five daily London newspapers, fifty-five periodicals, five provincial papers, as well as directories and timetables. Situations vacant sections from various newspapers would be posted outside the doors of this library at seven o' clock every morning. It is perhaps this use of the library in helping to find work that explains its popularity when this photograph was taken.

Event at Bethnal Green Library, children's section, 27 December 1956. The children gaze at the Christmas tree while the children's librarian, fourth from left, looks on.

The talent contest at Oxford House, Derbyshire Street, 31 October 1952. This was always a popular event. The mayor of Bethnal Green, Councillor Mrs B.L. Tate, JP, attended this contest. Oxford House was founded by members of Keble College Oxford in 1884. Their aim was to provide a settlement to give religious, social and educational services to the East End and to give graduates practical experience working in a needy area. The settlement was successful in this aim and by the 1930s a large number of leading Anglican churchmen had gained experience and valuable insight by working in Oxford House. Oxford House encouraged many clubs, but they all had a total ban on betting and beer. It is therefore no surprise that there was some resentment to what was seen as middle-class values being imposed on working class habits. One interesting irony was Ben Tillet, the union leader of the 1889 Dock Strike, who learnt some of his strategies, perhaps, by attending lectures at Oxford House, on Napoleon's strategy, in 1886-87. After the Second World War, Oxford House became mainly a community centre, the purpose it is serving in this photograph.

Bethnal Green Central Hall, Men's Fellowship, March 1931. The Central Hall in Approach Road began life as the Approach Road Wesleyan chapel. It became part of the Wesleyan East End Mission in 1927. This was a network of seven centres throughout East London. Following extensive reconstruction in 1929 it changed its name to Bethnal Green Central Hall. The men's fellowship was one of hundreds of highly popular meetings held weekly for men, women and children at the Mission's centres. The minister, Revd Robertson Ballard, is seventh from the left at the back of this photograph. The church survives, although due to war damage it has been completely rebuilt, as Bethnal Green Methodist church.

Bethnal Green Central Hall, Bethnal Green Sisterhood, 5 July 1952. The Sisterhood assemble before a trip to Eastbourne. The Sisterhood was initiated by Revd Thomas Stephenson, in 1878/79. The aim was to train women for mission work in the East End. It was located at 'Mewburn House', No. 84 Bonner Road, in 1890. The Probationer Sisters, as they were termed, would undertake domestic work until 10 a.m. and then exercise in Victoria Park for an hour, followed by two hours of lessons. However by the time of this photograph, the Sisterhood was more of a social club for women.

Daniel Street Women's Institute, Gossett Street, Open Week, 16-20 March, 1953. The dressmaking exhibit attracts attention. It was reported that twenty-one-year-old Vera had made her sun-suit at the institute and planned to wear it at the beach in Great Yarmouth during the coming summer. A wide variety of pursuits were demonstrated during the open week, including fencing, drama, metalwork, French conversation, cookery and dancing classes.

Fire station, Green Street, now Roman Road, looking from Globe Road, before the First World War. The fire station was built in 1889. There was accommodation on the eastern side of Globe road for an officer and six men and on the western side for two horses. The large doors were designed for horse-drawn appliances. The station was enlarged in 1907. A drill tower for training of firemen was built in 1912. This station was replaced by one built on the corner of Roman Road and Victoria Park Square in 1966-67. The building survives as a Buddhist centre.

Sarel House, Buckfast Street, 1960. This London County Council home for the elderly was opened in July 1960. The garden of Sarel House has within it Georg Ehrlick's 'faun with goose'. This bronze statue represents a goose trying to escape from the grip of a faun, a non-classical god. This statue forms part of a fountain, which flows into a mosaic pool with fish and plants.

Sarel House, Buckfast Street, 1960. Residents of Sarel House are passing the time knitting and chatting – possibly about some of the events depicted in this book!

Four
Places of Worship

The parish church of St Matthews, *c.* 1810. In 1743 an Act was passed which made Bethnal Green a separate parish from Stepney and St Matthews was consecrated in 1746. Nowadays this beautiful church is hidden from sight of passers-by in Bethnal Green Road because of the building of shops in this road. It recently received publicity as the place chosen for the funeral services of the Kray brothers, who spent their early days in the local area.

The parish church of St Matthews, late nineteenth century. By 1851 Bethnal Green had twelve Anglican churches, eleven parsonages, ten Church of England schools, twenty-two clergymen, 129 district visitors and 244 Sunday school teachers. Since its consecration the church has undergone much repair and rebuilding. Part of this rebuilding can be seen in effect with the addition of the cupola on the tower, added in 1860 during rebuilding, after a fire had devastated the interior of the church a year earlier.

St Jude's, Old Bethnal Green Road, c. 1905. This church was consecrated in 1846. One of its most active curates was Wilfred Davis, curate from 1892-96. He raised money for many worthy causes, including a soup kitchen in St Jude's Street and Old Bethnal Green Road. It was damaged by bombing in 1940 and later demolished.

St John's church, corner of Cambridge Heath Road and Green Street (later Roman Road), c. 1909. The church was consecrated in 1828, and the vicarage was built in 1852. The design of the church by Sir John Soane was controversial. The west tower with its cupola, which can be seen in the picture, was described as an 'object of low wit and vulgar abuse'. This church has recently undergone refurbishment and has seen many events over its long history, including the wedding of the author's parents.

Pott Street, Congregational church, Bethnal Green Road, c. 1910. The spire of this church, which flourished in the 1850s, being the only congregational place of worship in the area, measured 125ft and was removed in 1946 because of wartime damage. This church was probably founded by Revd Thomas Walton in 1662. The church was built on its present site in 1850 and was known as the Bethnal Green Road Congregational church. It became the United Reformed church in 1965 and the Bethnal Green United Reformed church in 1974, when the merging of Congregational and Presbyterian churches took place.

A ticket to a performance by the Canadian Jubilee Singers at Bethnal Green Road Congregational church, Pott Street, 1884. The purpose of this concert was to raise money for the Theological Institute in Canada, which wished to train and educate black men of African descent for mission work in Africa.

SPECIAL INVITATION TICKET.

BETHNAL GREEN-RD. CONGREGATIONAL CHURCH,

CORNER OF POTT STREET,

WEDNESDAY, APRIL 23rd, 1884,

SELECTION OF JUBILEE MUSIC

BY THE

Canadian Jubilee Singers

Accompanied by the Rht. Rev. BISHOP DISNEY.

Doors open at 7·30 p.m., to commence at 8.0 p.m.

Collection on behalf of proposed Theological Institute in Canada for the education of young black men for African Mission Work.

St Peter's church, St Peter's Avenue, c. 1969. This was the first of the Blomfield churches. Bishop Blomfield, the Bishop of London, was concerned with the spiritual destitution of the East End, so to rectify this problem he embarked on a scheme to raise money for a number of churches. However funds were limited and he decided to concentrate the building of new churches where he thought they were needed most. So ten new churches were planned for Bethnal Green, each dedicated to an apostle. The foundation stone was laid in 1840 and the ceremony was met with some hostility by the locals, who jeered and released an oxen, causing some disruption to the ceremony.

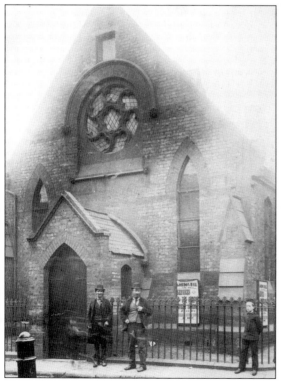

'Cripples' church, Bonner Street, late nineteenth century. This church was run by the National Children's Home in Bonner Street and may have been its chapel. The nickname it has acquired presumably relates in particular to the condition of the children, who sought religious and charitable relief within its walls.

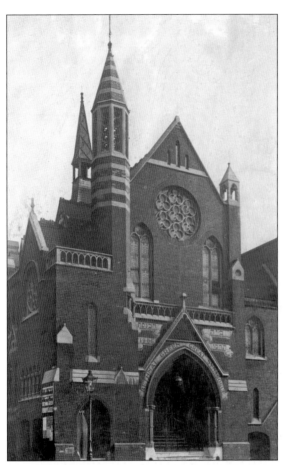

Bethnal Green Great Synagogue, Chance Street, in the 1930s. The date on this synagogue refers to its foundation in 1906. This synagogue stood on the site of a former Baptist chapel and was a member of the Federation of the Synagogues. This federation, founded in 1887, aimed amongst other things to create a standard of public worship among its member synagogues, all of which were in East London. This building was damaged by bombing during the Second World War and was rebuilt. The new building accommodated 350 men and 100 ladies and included flats for a Rabbi and a Chazan. The synagogue closed in 1984.

St Barnabas' church, corner of Roman Road and Grove Road, 1865. The foundation stone laying ceremony of the 'Union church'. This church, primarily concerned with Baptist worship, originated from St Luke's Mission run by St Simon Zelotes; it was bought by the Baptist Association in 1867 and sold to the Church of England a year later. This church then became St Barnabas', being consecrated in 1870.

St Barnabas' church, corner of Roman Road and Grove Road, 1900s. The impressive spire was removed in 1947 after it was damaged by bombing during the war. Much of the church was rebuilt in 1956-57.

St Andrew's church, Viaduct Street, c. 1850. The Parish was formed in 1843. The church ran a mission in Cambridge Road. Many of the slum houses nearby were demolished in the 1950s, while the church itself was demolished and united with St Matthews in 1958. The site of the church was incorporated into Weaver's Fields.

Episcopal Jews chapel, Palestine Place, c. 1880. The London Society for Promoting Christianity among the Jews built the Episcopal Jews chapel and its associated buildings, called Palestine Place, in around 1836. This was situated on the eastern side of Cambridge Road between Cambridge Road and Russia Lane. The chapel for 1,200 people was opened in 1814, but was demolished in 1895 to make way for the Bethnal Green Infirmary and Hospital. The bell tower from the old Episcopal Jews chapel survived on the nurses quarters of the Infirmary until it was considered unsafe and demolished in October 1982. The Infirmary was demolished six years later, and the font and wall monuments of the chapel were taken to Christ Church, Spitalfields.

Five
Pubs

Old and New, The City of Paris, No. 178 Old Ford Road, 1968. The original City of Paris stood on the junction of Old Ford Road and Mace Street. Mace Street can be seen between the old City of Paris, which was about to be demolished, and the new City of Paris on the right of the picture, which was built at 74 Bonner Street. The tower blocks in the background belong to Cranbrook Estate, and it was the building of this estate that resulted in Mace Street being cleared and the old pub being demolished. It had stood on this site since the turn of the twentieth century.

Salmon & Ball, Cambridge Road, Bethnal Green. E.

Looking west, an open-topped bus goes past the Salmon and Ball on the corner of Cambridge Heath Road and Bethnal Green Road in the early twentieth century. This is one of the most famous pubs in the area. The salmon in the name may be an indicator of salmon being caught in the Thames, while the ball was a symbol of the Roman Emperor Constantine the Great and may be derived from Huguenot links, as silk weavers adopted this sign as silk originally came from the east. However, the name may also be connected with the coat of arms of one Thomas Elton whose residence was between it and the City. When the footballer Bobby Moore became joint licensee, there arose some controversy when in 1978 he changed the pub name to Tipples. In 1991 the name was changed back to the original one. On 6 December 1769 the execution of John Doyle and John Valline took place on the crossroads outside the pub. Their crime was involvement in the Cutter's Riots whereby weavers, who cut silk from looms, were on strike for higher wages. They were hung for the crimes of rioting and machine breaking.

Duke of Wellington, No. 29 Three Colts Lane, looking north, *c.* 1916. Another public house named after the famous victor at the Battle of Waterloo, who later became Prime Minister. Twenty-one pubs of this name were serving the needs of thirsty customers in London at this time – this pub stood between Violet Street and Primrose Street. In the late 1920s Allen and Hanbury's took over this pub to use as a store.

Above left: Drawing of the Red Deer public house, No. 393 Cambridge Heath Road, 1878. The Red Deer underwent alterations in 1878, and this illustration by an unknown artist is a depiction of the pub after these alterations. The pub first appears in the trade directories in 1855. *Above right*: The Britannia, No. 12 Chilton Street, pre-1970. James Ayton is listed in the trade directory as a beer retailer at this address in 1867. The building dates from the 1890s.

The Marquis of Cornwallis, No. 304 Bethnal Green Road, October 1969. Vallance Road is on the right. The pub is arguably named after Charles Cornwallis, the first Marquis of Cornwallis (1738-1805), a soldier and governor general of India. More famously, perhaps, he commanded troops during the American War of Independence and surrendered at Yorktown. The pub can be traced back to 1870.

Bonner Arms, No. 1 Tagg Street, viewed from the south east, October 1957. Tagg Street is on the left, Bonner Street on the right. A beer retailer's shop can be traced at this address in 1897. In 1958 the pub and Tagg Street, previously known as John Street until July 1874, was cleared to make way for the Cranbrook Estate.

The Birdcage, No. 80 Columbia Road, photographed from the north west, October 1957. The name of this pub is a reminder that the people of Bethnal Green have long been associated with the practise of keeping as well as trading caged birds in the area. A pub of this name has been here since 1760. In 1973 the pub underwent a somewhat colourful renovation and redecoration with gilded birds spotlighted in rainbow colours suspended high above the bar. This decoration was changed again in 1981, when another bird theme was taken up; this time stuffed birds decorated the bar.

The Shakespeare, Bethnal Green Road, in the 1980s. There has been a beer retailer on this site since at least 1845. The Shakespeare public house first appears in the trade directory in 1954 when the landlady was Mrs Emily Coleman who gained a license for spirits at this time. Before this date she had run the beer retailers on this site since the 1940s. To the right of this pub is Bethnal Green police station, which has in recent times been replaced by one in Victoria Park Square. The police station building is now occupied by the offices of a housing association.

The Prince Albert, No. 61 Old Ford
Road, corner of Russia Lane,
September 1954. The Prince Albert
first got its license to sell spirits in
1954; before this date and since at least
1889 it had been a beer retailer. Russia
Lane appears to be derived from Rushy,
a name associated with this lane in the
early eighteenth century. This name
has echoes of the rural past of Bethnal
Green before industrialisation. Only six
years after it was granted a license to
sell spirits, the pub was cleared to make
way for the grounds of James Campbell
House. The date of 1666 is the
establishment date of the pub's supplier
of beer, Truman's Brewery.

A grocer's shop at No. 77 Mape Street,
November 1955, formerly the Anchor
Hope public house. Although the date
stone states 1899, a beer retailers had
been at this address from around 1873
until the premises were converted into
a Chandlers' shop in around 1926. This
area was included in a London County
Council compulsory purchase order in
1955. Park land, in the form of
Weaver's Fields, now replaces much of
Mape Street.

The Rising Sun, 248 Globe Road, with Roman Road on the left, in the 1960s. This public house was built on part of a field known as Turnip Field. The Rising Sun can be traced back to the mid 1800s, and it ceased trading as a pub in 1966.

The Old George, 379 Bethnal Green Road, 1885. Everyone seems keen to appear in this photograph. This was one of the oldest pubs in the borough, the original building appears on Rocque's map of 1741-45, and was probably named after George II. It was first recorded in an account book of the brewers Truman, Hanbury and Buxtons in 1742 as receiving beer from them. The name visible above the door of the pub is that of H.J.K. Balls, who entered the licensed trade at the age of twenty-two. His son, Austin Balls, became a wine merchant and by 1929 Ye Olde George sold only registered wines. The pub was renovated in 1974.

Opposite, below: The Cabin Public House, No. 2 Quinn's Building, Russia Lane, September 1954. This public house formed part of a block of flats with flats built above it.

The Palm Tree public house, Numbers 24-26 Palm Street, pre-1970. The Palm Tree was established in 1861 at the same time as Palm Street. The streets either side of this pub are Palm Street and Lessada Street.

The landlord and friends enjoying a rest and a pint while clearing up bomb damage at the Approach Tavern, Approach Road, 1941. This area was bombed in several raids in April 1941. A high explosive bomb fell in Approach Road on the night of the 19/20 April 1941, causing a large crater and partially demolishing the pub. The pub was repaired and is still in existence today.

Six

Bethnal Green and the Second World War

A bombsite next to No. 164 Grove Road, fenced off with the billboard advertising Bethnal Green Warship Week 21-28 March 1942. On 7 September 1940 London saw the beginning of the Blitz and from then until 24 September raids were constant. In this period ninety-five high explosive bombs of varying sizes, from 50-1,000 kg, two parachute mines and countless incendiary bombs fell in Bethnal Green. Bombed sites like the one shown in the above photograph became an all too common sight.

Moore House, Roman Road, 1941, showing blast damage from a 1,000 kg bomb that fell at the junction of Roman Road and Victoria Park Square on the night of 19/20 April 1941. This bomb destroyed the Falcon pub and badly damaged Bethnal Green Estate. To the left of the two women talking is the new sign for Roman Road, above which is the old sign for Green Street, which has been crossed out. Above the women's heads there is a union jack defiantly draped across the railings.

Cyprus Street, c. 1941. The pockmarked walls indicate the force of the blast from a bomb. A family stand outside their bombed-out home, ready to look to a better future. This attitude was typical of the area during the war, after all what else could one do but carry on?

Approach Road, Bishops Way corner, April 1941. The result of the blast from a bomb that hit the London Chest Hospital, located on the opposite side of the road, on the night of 19/20 April 1941. This street was cleared and Reynold's House was built there in 1953.

Children at Russia Lane allotments, near Bishops Way, c. 1942. Russia Lane was partially a bombsite, which was cleared and made into allotments. These allotments provided fresh vegetables including peas, potatoes and cabbages. The children pictured here would work on the allotments with the aid of tools borrowed from the fire department and would watch over the allotments through the day. The Chief Warden of Bethnal Green, Sir Wyndham Deedes, had the original idea of creating gardens on bombed sites.

Bethnal Green Town Hall, 1942. The Cambridge Heath Road entrance of the Town Hall, another picture taken during Bethnal Green warship week. The Town Hall escaped damage and had many near misses during the war and remained in operation. The control room of the essential service of Air-Raid Precautions was located in the basement of the Town Hall.

Railway Bridge, Bethnal Green Road, looking west, March, 1942. After Hitler's attempt to bomb the country into submission, life in Bethnal Green carried on as near to normal as possible. The sign calls on the people to help the war effort – one of several fund raising efforts during the war in the borough. To the right can be seen a section of Paradise Row where the famous boxer Daniel Mendoza once lived. The writing on the bridge referring to the 'Oldest Inn in the District', refers to the Old George public house.

The interior of St Simon Zelotes church, Morpeth Street, after bombing on the night of the 20/21 October 1943. The Reverend H.R. Peerless surveys the bomb damage. This church had been in existence since 1844, but the extensive bomb damage would prove fatal to the church and it was later demolished.

Victoria Park, Congregational chapel, Approach Road, undated. The interior of the chapel is in ruins with a collapsed roof – one can only imagine the consequences if the church had been full at the time. The area surrounding the church was heavily bombed on 19 March and the night of the 19/20 April 1941, so the photograph presumably shows the aftermath of one of these raids.

Interior of St Matthews parish church, gutted by bomb damage, c. 1946. A temporary church was built within the walls of the old one and dedicated on 27 November 1954. In 1957 it was decided to rebuild the church and Anthony Lewis was appointed as architect. The temporary church was demolished in 1960 and services were then held in the parish room and at St James the Great. On 15 July 1961 the present church was re-consecrated. In 1972 it was restored further and redecorated.

Bethnal Green Central Library, the interior filled with rubble after bombing, 7 September 1940. This destruction did not stop the librarians serving the people of the borough – Bethnal Green Library opened the first shelter library in Bethnal Green Tube Shelter on 21 October 1941. This was open until 6 February 1942, and was only 15ft square, with a choice of 4,000 books.

Globe Road, *c.* 1941. Smashed and buried ice cream carts belonging to Benjamin Rood, of 279 Globe Road, after an air raid. One can see that the ice cream vendors offered various sizes of tub, up to 6d for the largest. This would have been a luxury in wartime.

Workers search through the bomb damage around Columbia Buildings, Columbia Market, 1941. On Sunday 8 September 1940 a 50kg bomb entered the ventilation shaft of the large public shelter in Columbia Market, causing extensive casualties. The work undertaken by the workers searching through bombed buildings was hazardous. Civilian defence rescuers were involved in heavy rescue during the war, of these one was killed and three seriously injured, and of those undertaking light rescue, ten suffered injuries.

Columbia Buildings, May 1941.
Workers sifting through the
wreckage of part of Columbia
Buildings caused by bombing on the
night of 10/11 May 1941. The
salvaged remains of someone's house
can be seen piled in the foreground,
while in the background pictures
still hang over the fireplace of an
exposed sitting room that had been
destroyed.

Pedley Street, May 1941. Eckersley
Street is on the right. Just one
example of the extensive damage to
properties that occurred in Bethnal
Green during the war. From 1940-
1945 2,233 houses were destroyed,
893 were made uninhabitable, 2,457
were seriously damaged and 16,117
were slightly damaged. To this list of
statistics must be added the
postscript that every house was
home to a family, and the impact on
them of losing their homes cannot
be measured in numbers.

Entrance of Bethnal Green tube station, c. 1943. After a lull in bombing in Bethnal Green a disaster was to occur here which cost the lives of 173 men, women and children. On the evening of 3 March 1943 sirens sounded and people made their way to the shelter in Bethnal Green tube station. Londoners were expecting reprisals after the RAF had launched a 300 bomber raid against Berlin and the BBC had reported it on that day. Suddenly a salvo of rockets was fired from a battery in Victoria Park. This noise sounded to many like bombs falling and people rushed to the shelter. What happened next is subject to speculation, but it is generally agreed that a woman holding a baby slipped on the stairs which led down to the shelter and people fell on top. There was soon a crush of bodies five to six deep with people still pushing forward, anxious to get to safety. Within ninety seconds, 173 people were dead, sixty-two of them children. The sole cause of death for all these people was suffocation. It took three hours to clear all the casualties and the Home Guard and the Scouts helped to remove the bodies. An official enquiry blamed panic as the cause of the disaster, however the entrance to the station had no handrails, no crush barrier and was lit by a single twenty-five watt bulb. Handrails were soon fixed to the stairs after the disaster. A commemorative plaque above the stairwell now marks where this avoidable disaster occurred. No bombs fell on Bethnal Green on that night. In 1975 ATV made a film of the disaster focusing on the fictitious Bell family, it was filmed in and around Bethnal Green and was directed and produced by John Goldschmidt. The film was titled after the popular song It's a Lovely Day Tomorrow.

Bethnal Green Town Hall Home Guard parading past Bethnal Green Gardens, *c.* 1941. The Home Guard was formed in May 1940 and was dissolved on 31 December 1944. At its peak in 1942 the Home Guard had over one and a half million men. Members of the Home Guard, although not called upon to defend the country from invasion, did occasionally serve on anti-aircraft batteries during the Blitz and undertook many other duties for national security. A year before war was declared, Bethnal Green was undertaking preparations in case of war – these included digging trenches in Bethnal Green Gardens for use as air-raid shelters, signalling the start of war preparations in Bethnal Green. By the end of September 1938 66,828 gas masks had been issued.

St Peter's Avenue, 17 June 1942. The Queen visits the East End. Councillor Sanders is to the right of the Queen and following them are the mayor and mayoress, the Town Clerk and Councillor Tate. Every vantage point is taken up in order to try to get a glimpse of the Queen, including perching on top of the air-raid shelter.

Bethnal Green Wardens are attending a service in 1940, Sir Wyndham Deedes is third from the left. During the war the wardens had to deal with some 269 major incidents, caused by eighty tons of missiles falling in the borough. One Bethnal Green warden was killed, three seriously injured and seventeen minor injuries during the war.

Victory Day Party, Jesus Hospital Estate, 1945. The generation that would see significant changes in post-war Bethnal Green pose for a photograph to celebrate victory. In 1868 the Improved Industrial Dwellings Company acquired nine acres of land belonging to Barnet Jesus Hospital Charity and constructed terraces. This was the last of the company's estates to be sold. The Greater London Council purchased part of the area in 1970 and in 1979-80 a Hackney firm, who refurbished the terraces, bought the rest of the estate.

Victory Day Parade, 8 June 1946. Military vehicles going along Cambridge Heath Road as part of the mechanised procession to celebrate the end of the Second World War. Field Marshall Viscount Montgomery, wearing a black beret, was reported to have received the loudest cheers as this parade passed through streets in Stepney and Bethnal Green on its way to the City via the Tower of London. Field Marshall Alexander, Marshall Viscount Portal and Admiral Lord Mountbatten also took part in this part of the parade. This parade, described as the biggest event of the day, avoided the rain that fell later in the day, meaning that some street parties that had been planned were held under cover.

Bethnal Green Library, November 1950. The unveiling of a stained glass window by the mayor councillor A.G. Clark in memory of the war dead. The number of civilian casualties in the borough was 555 people killed and 400 seriously injured.

The mayor takes the salute on Remembrance Day, 1951. Marching past the borough's peace memorial outside Bethnal Green Library. Those taking part in the parade included, among others, the Salvation Army band, nurses from Bethnal Green Hospital, local units of the British Legion, Civil Defence, St John Ambulance Brigade and Women's Voluntary Service.

Percy Holman MP unveiling the war memorial outside Bethnal Green Library, 13 November 1960. Observing on the left is the mayor of Bethnal Green, councillor G.M. Browne.

Bethnal Green Warden's Association annual reunion, 26 April 1952. The organization had a membership of over 100 and this picture records an award presentation. The trophies were presented to winners of indoor sporting events.

Seven

Industry, Shops and Markets

A Weavers' race starting from Type Street, c. 1900. The result of the race has been lost in the mists of time. A book by Sir Frank Warner published in 1914 stated that there were forty-six weavers' workshops in Cranbrook and Alma (later Doric) Road. When the trade finally declined many of these men would have gone to the docks in search of work. Although these men seem to be in physically good shape, this was not the norm for those involved in this industry – the long working days of typically twelve to fourteen hours were coupled with humid conditions in the workshops. The large windows of these workshops were deliberately sealed to keep the rooms humid and prevent the delicate silk thread from breaking, however this made chest problems common with weavers.

Engraving from *Illustrated London News*, October 1863. A room occupied by a tailor and his family at 10 Hollybush Place. An inquest into the death of a child in this area during this period concluded that the cause was blood poisoning brought about by the sheer filth of the area in which he lived. This picture shows only one chair in the room and everyone else is on the floor, with the ironing board at the tailor's feet. This type of cramped workshop was common. Many families worked together in this trade as they did in many other trades, such as matchbox-making and clothes-peg making in similar cramped conditions. You worked to survive; if you didn't work you didn't eat.

Mrs Stanley Baldwin visits Mrs Mary Waite, 8 April 1930. Mrs Waite was one of the last weavers of Huguenot descent still working in Bethnal Green. She is seen here in her house at No. 45 Cranbrook Street. She was the wife of Charles Waite, another weaver of Huguenot descent. One of the most famous weavers who lived in the Bethnal Green area was George Doree, who wove the cloth for the coronation robe of Edward VII. Doree's house was cleared for the Cranbrook Estate.

Day's Birdcage shop, No. 198 Cambridge Heath Road, 1905. A sign in the window reads 'Budgies boarded during your holidays.' Mayfield House is now situated on part of this site.

Bird Market, Club Row, 1904. The interest in gardening and bird-keeping are a reminder of the influence of a past Huguenot society on the area. Bird fancying, and breeding canaries, was a favourite activity of the weavers. There were matches between singing birds held in taverns in Hare Street, and visitors to Bethnal Green in the 1840s would often remark on the aviaries in the parish. One of the best poultry clubs in the country was said to meet at the Bethnal Green Men's Institute in the 1930s.

Numbers 82-88 Sclater Street, *c.* 1955. Of particular note is No. 82 Kemp's 'the largest pineapple retailer in England'. This street, like the previously mentioned Birdcage public house, serves to highlight the importance at one time of bird trading in the area. In 1943, eight out of fifteen properties on the south side of Sclater Street were involved with bird dealing directly or indirectly in activities such as birdcage making. No. 82 was listed in the 1953 and 1954 trade directories as being occupied by Mrs L.R. Hutchinson, a bird dealer.

Crutchlow's, No. 1 Russia Lane, *c.* 1910. A general goods shop well known in the area. On the left is Elizabeth Martin, in the doorway is Mary Crutchlow (née Smith) and on the right George Crutchlow.

H. Outram Dining Rooms, Hackney Road, c. 1902. The owner, Mr Henry Outram, poses for this photograph with his wife and staff. One can see from the notices in the window that a pot of tea was available for 2d, and if you fancied a steamed pudding as well it would cost you 4d extra.

Row of shops in Cambridge Heath Road, east side, c. 1932. To the left can be seen Martha Court. This stretch of Cambridge Heath Road was situated between Bishop's Road and Wadeson Street. In 1932, No. 268 was a dining room owned by H.M. Shorey, while next door could be found Miss Elizabeth Curry's chandler's shop.

Milk deliveries departing from Morgan's Dairy and Provision Shop, 229 Green Street, c. 1920. Morgan's is an example of the Welsh connection with the London dairy trade. Welsh cattle drovers would bring beef cattle to Smithfield market; these men would often find work for Welsh women from impoverished backgrounds, who in time would work in the dairy trade and in turn be joined by relatives. By 1881 the Welsh were running a quarter of London's dairies.

Hackney Road, Cambridge Heath, c. 1910. The building on the left is the Chandler's Wiltshire brewery. A brewery was here by the 1860s and was rebuilt and extended in 1871 and 1893. No. 505 Hackney Road was registered in May 1900 as Chandler & Co. to acquire the business of George Charles Porter and William Henry Disseldorff. In December 1910 the brewery and thirty-five public houses were offered for sale. By 1911, a half interest in the brewery and public house was taken up by Charrington & Co. The brewery had stopped operating from this site by 1919.

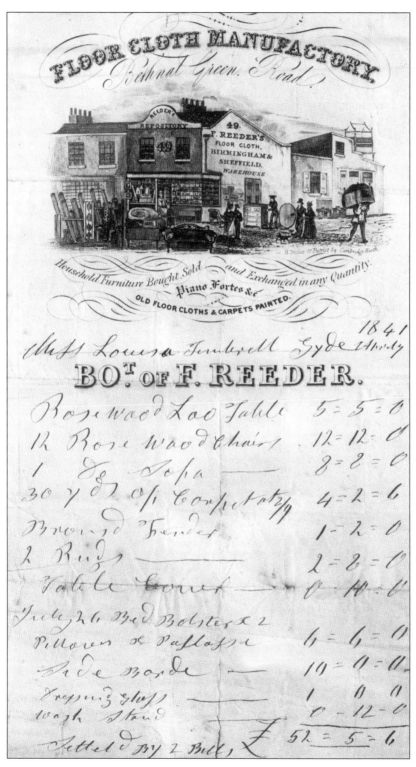

An invoice from F. Reeder's Floor Cloth Manufactory, Bethnal Green Road, dated 7 April 1841.

William Westover & Son Ltd, No. 13 Wood Street, c. 1910. Thomas and Rosina Westover had been in the sack and bag business since 1889. Their son William started the business in Wood Street in 1909. Pictured are William and Mary Westover with their children, Mary Ann who is holding Violet (1910-98) and seated left to right are Elizabeth Lilian (b. 1905), William (1902-1976), who seems to be wishing he was elsewhere, Rosina Mary Ann (b. 1903) and Albert (1905-1987). No. 13 Wood Street was destroyed during the war and later rebuilt when it became Nos 5-9 Wood Close, Cheshire Street. The cloth-sack trade died out in the early 1970s due to the use of plastic and paper sacking. The premises were converted into flats. Elizabeth Lilian is the only surviving member of this group and will celebrate her ninety-seventh birthday in December 2002.

No. 48 Cambridge Heath Road, October 1935. This hairdressers was owned by Mrs Laura Spumberg in 1935. The Spumberg family had been operating this hairdressers since around 1909.

J.F. List, No. 418 Bethnal Green Road, special bakers of Dr Allinson's bread by appointment, c. 1906. In 1908 this shop was occupied by Philip Frederick List, baker. Dr Allinson, a dietician, believed that eating wholemeal bread every day was vital to enjoying good health as it was more nutritious than white bread. In the 1880s–1900s he issued certificates to bakers of quality wholemeal bread to display in their windows and increase trade. Dr Allinson had one share in the Natural Food Company which milled wholemeal flour at 24a Patriot Square, near List's bakery.

Porret's, No. 79 Cyprus Street, on the corner of Cyprus Place, in the 1950s. This general store, named after its occupier Sidney Porrett, sold groceries, provisions, confectionery and minerals. Examples which can be glimpsed in the window include Omo soap powder, tinned goods and a sign for Lyons cakes. This type of store, selling a wide range of goods, has all but disappeared today due to competition from supermarkets. This shop had a somewhat short existence from 1953-1958, being succeeded by a grocer's store occupied by C. Purdy.

Jack Finch Ltd, cabinet manufacturers, No. 49 Bethnal Green Road, 3 October 1957. In the 1861 census there can be traced 2,563 people in Bethnal Green connected with the furniture-making business. In 1872 there was 121 cabinet makers, chair makers and upholstering establishments in Bethnal Green, many of which were located along Bethnal Green Road, with some eight timber yards along this road in the 1870s. Bethnal Green was a prime location for those involved in the furniture trade as cheap imported wood was available, brought in via the Regents Canal.

R. Libling General Cabinet Makers Supplies, 72 Hare Street, c. 1923-26. Standing outside the shop are Malcolm and Ray Libling, the son and daughter of Rebecca Libling. This shop presumably supplied materials to the large cabinet making industry in Bethnal Green.

Phillip Lowry, No. 24 Brick Lane, *c.* 1890. Lowry was a greengrocer and fishmonger selling, as it says on the hoarding, 'fish and potatoes'. It also appears, from the baskets outside the shop, that he sold chickens.

Bethnal Green Starch Works, Numbers 5-13 Old Ford Road, *c.* 1910. The man standing next to the horse and cart is Mr Frobisher, the foreman of the starch works. J.J. Colman of Norwich, the mustard manufacturer, bought this factory in the 1860s and manufactured starch here from July 1873. The factory closed in 1916, by which time it had expanded to Numbers 5-13 Old Ford Road. The Bethnal Green Borough Council purchased the starch works in 1923 and demolished it to make way for York Hall baths.

Allen and Hanbury's factories, Three Colts Lane, 1913. This pharmaceutical and manufacturing chemist originated in an apothecary's shop off Lombard Street in 1715. Allen and Hanbury's acquired part of Letchford Buildings, which had partially been used as a match factory, in Three Colts Lane in 1874 and due to growing demand enlarged the warehouse in 1881. The factory also manufactured surgical instruments. A new factory was built after earlier wartime bomb damage in May 1918, but this factory again suffered more bomb damage in the Second World War in 1940. The company merged with the Glaxo Group in 1958, and from 1967 until its closure in 1982 the building was used purely for administration.

Illustration from the *Illustrated London News*, 27 November 1858, showing the large gas holder at the Imperial Gas Company's works, No. 110 Emma Street. This company was the main supplier of gas to Bethnal Green, later merging with Gas, Light and Coke Company in 1887. These holders were hit on the morning of the 16 November 1940 with fragments of a high explosive bomb, and not surprisingly caught fire. By the late 1970s North Sea Gas had made the holders redundant, yet they remain as an impressive relic of historical architecture.

Columbia Market, the Quadrangle, illustration from 1869. This market was conceived by Baroness Angela Burdett-Coutts, whose aim was to move costermongers from the streets, as their Sunday marketing was seen to attract undesirable elements. This elaborate gothic structure was designed by H.A. Darbishire and opened in 1869 at a cost of £200,000. The most expensive materials were used in the construction of this market – teak, granite and Irish marble. The market had space for thirty-six shops and 673 spaces in the galleries and quadrangles for other traders. The market resembled a cathedral and indeed every fifteen minutes the bells in the clock tower would chime a hymn tune. The local population, however, preferred the street stalls, and the costers consequently also preferred the streets. The market was given back to Baroness Burdett-Coutts in 1874 and was reopened again in 1884 as workshops. A scheme was undertaken by de-mobbed servicemen in 1919 to re-establish the market, but this failed. In the Second World War the market served as an air-raid shelter. This architecturally splendid building was demolished in 1958 to make way for council flats.

Columbia Road flower market, 1980. The flower market probably originated as an offshoot from the Columbia market, and follows a tradition of flower trading which began in London in the 1830s. Depending on the season every type of flower is available to buy here.

A busy morning in Bethnal Green Road Market, looking east, 1968. It appears that there was still a market for fireguards in this period. The church, which is partly obscured by the stalls, is St James the Great. This scene of shoppers is one that Bethnal Green Road Market has witnessed since the early nineteenth century.

Club Row Market, Cygnet Street, January 1932, viewed from the Bethnal Green Road. This cycle market offered every spare you could wish for.

Selling puppies in Club Row Market, 1953. The practice of selling animals in Club Row market was banned in 1983 following a long campaign of protest. The author remembers as a boy visiting this market and peering into crates which held puppies, and pestering his parents for one. The children in this photograph are probably doing the same thing some twenty-five years earlier!

Jellied eel stall, Sclater Street, Club Row Market, 1956. One of the foods most associated with the East End, seen here being dished up in the market.

London Co-operative Society, Numbers 124-26 Roman Road, 1959, this was the first in the area. This photograph was taken a year or so before the shops were cleared to make way for a market place for retail street vendors. The butcher's is on the left and the grocer's on the right. On the right the street name Green Street can be seen crossed off and the new Roman Road name replacing it.

Newman's Automobile Agents, Cambridge Heath Road, November 1956. These showrooms were situated opposite Bethnal Green Hospital and extended under the railway arch to Clare Street.

Eight

The People
of Bethnal Green

A happy day: a wedding group pictured on the roof of No. 109 Leopold Buildings, Columbia Road, 1926. The marriage of Percy H.C. Puttock and Ethel Hill was solemnized in St Leonard's church, Shoreditch. The bride and bridesmaids' dresses were made by the bride's sister. Percy H.C. Puttock and Ethel Hill had lived next door to each other in Columbia Buildings before their marriage, Percy at No. 105 and Ethel at No. 108. After marriage they lived together at No. 109. Ethel was still living at this address in 1969 but Percy had gone by 1945, possibly a casualty of war.

Illustration of an East End Flower Show from *An Illustrated Journal of Sunday Reading*, August 1873. By following the directions given in the article that accompanies this illustration, and by consulting an 1872 Ordinance Survey map, one can deduce that the flower show took place at the New Nichol Row Ragged School, which opened in 1866.

Queen Mary with Brigadier General Sir Wyndam Deedes, in the background on the far right, visits gardens in Bethnal Green, July 1935. Members of the Bethnal Green Gardens Guild were visited by the Queen, who was described as an 'expert gardener'. She visited many gardens, including two plots belonging to George Bryant of Albert Street, a brewer worker. When news spread that the Queen was in the area many people hurried to the street to catch a glimpse of her. At Devonshire Street the Queen stopped her car and she chatted to women in the street, including, it was stated, some who still had curlers in their hair.

Queen Mary is pictured departing from the Excelsior Cinema, Mansford Street, May 1928. Oxford House acquired this site in 1898 on a lease for eighty years. The building contained two swimming baths, which were floored over in winter for concerts and meetings. In 1921 the Hall was converted into the Excelsior Cinema. Lectures were still given on Sunday afternoons and one night a month was devoted to opera. The dual purpose of this building was highlighted when the Queen visited the area to view a production by the Oxford House Choral Society of *Il Pagliacci* held at the cinema and the film *Chang*. Queen Mary proceeded to Oxford House after spending two hours in the building. The mayor of Bethnal Green, M.H. Seymour, accompanied her through a guard of honour formed by some of the performers of the opera production. The Excelsior was demolished in 1969.

Smart's Picture Palace, Numbers 281-285 Bethnal Green Road, before alterations in the 1930s. Smart's was named after its proprietor George Smart. The cinema was built in 1912 and altered in 1920 before becoming the Rex in around 1939.

The Rex Cinema, Bethnal Green Road, around 1939, after alterations by George Cole, arguably the leading cinema designer of the day. When the Rex was altered from Smart's it seated 865. The cinema was renamed the Essoldo in 1949 and closed in 1964, becoming firstly a bingo hall and then a warehouse.

Staff of the Odeon Cinema, No. 93 Cambridge Heath Road, pictured at its opening in October 1949.

Foresters, opening as the Odeon Cinema, No. 93 Cambridge Heath Road, October 1949. People outside struggle to get a glimpse of the movie star Dirk Bogarde in conversation with the mayor and mayoress. The site of the Odeon had a proven track record of being the place for entertainment in Bethnal Green. On the site once stood the Foresters Music Hall, which in 1893 could seat 3,000 people, all of which would be occupied when renowned music hall artists, such as Dan Leno, would appear. These shows would play on a Monday, as it was the costermonger's day off. The history of entertainment on this site goes back further than this. The Royal Foresters Music Hall was on the site of the earlier Artichoke Music Hall, which opened in 1800, and after reconstruction undertaken in 1891, changed its name to the Foresters Music Hall. It then became a cinema in 1910, becoming the New Lyric Cinema in 1916 and closing a year later. The cinema reopened as the Foresters in 1925 and closed in 1947. The cinema was reopened as the Odeon in October 1949 and lasted eleven years until its closure in 1960. A part of the entertainment history of Bethnal Green disappeared when the site was redeveloped and new flats were built there after the cinema's closure.

Illustration from *The Pictorial World of Bethnal Green Gardens*, June 1875. This illustration shows St John's church and Bethnal House. It was around here that probably the earliest 'Bethnal Greeners' lived. By the end of the sixteenth century this green was surrounded by mansions owned by courtiers and merchants from the City of London. In 1678 this area was part of Poor's Land. Thomas Rider and others who lived around the green bought eleven acres to stop building development and let some out as farmland. This land was in 1690 settled in trust for the poor. This scheme may have been designed to encourage the gentry to build in the area while stopping others. This theory grows stronger when one considers that in the period of the seventeenth century much of Bethnal Green was still open country. Impending development was not a threat. Bethnal Green Gardens still exists today as a reminder of this open country and possibly the wishes of seventeenth-century gentry to keep this rural idyll for their own pleasure.

Opening of York Hall Public Baths by the Duke and Duchess of York, 5 November 1929. The Public Hall and Baths, named after the Duke and Duchess of York, later King George VI and the Queen Mother, were designed by A.E. Darby in a neo-Georgian style. The red-brick building incorporated two swimming pools, Turkish, vapour and electric baths, and washhouses. York Hall has undergone much refurbishment over the years. The first-class swimming baths were converted into an assembly hall in around 1950. In the 1960s many other changes took place – a large swimming pool was built; the remaining swimming pool became a public hall, and the washhouse was converted into a bar and kitchen. York Hall is perhaps more famous outside Bethnal Green for being a venue for boxing and often appears on television in this capacity.

The public and machine laundry at York Hall Baths in the 1950s.

Entrance to Meath Gardens, undated. The emblem above the gateway indicates that this was originally the site of Victoria Park Cemetery opened in 1845. The Metropolitan Public Gardens Association acquired Victoria Park Cemetery in 1891. Tombstones were set against the walls and Meath Gardens, named after the chairman of the Metropolitan Public Gardens Association, the Earl of Meath, was laid out. The Duke of York, later King George V, officially opened it in 1894. One of the most famous people to be buried in the former cemetery was King Cole, an aborigine, who was part of the first Australian cricket team, an all-Aboriginal squad, to tour England. King Cole died in June 1868 after contracting tuberculosis.

Bethnal Green Museum, Cambridge Road, 1872. The museum's first collections consisted of food, animal products, and art, including for its first three years a collection from Sir Richard Wallace (which went on to form the Wallace collection in Marylebone). It was designed to spread 'a knowledge of science and art among the poorer classes'. After the First World War the museum became an art museum with a children's section. In 1974 the museum specialised in childhood. The author remembers as a child gazing longingly at the collections of toy soldiers and being in awe of a samurai warrior's armour – he can sometimes still be found today reliving his childhood wandering around the exhibits!

Arrival of the Prince of Wales at Bethnal Green Museum for its opening, June 1872, from *The Illustrated London News*. This museum, now known as the Bethnal Green Museum of Childhood, was built with a prefabricated iron structure by Charles Young & Co., nicknamed 'the Brompton boilers', and first served as a temporary home for its parent museum, the Victoria and Albert Museum, in 1856. The fountain depicted in this illustration was designed by J. Thomas, and measured an impressive 30ft high and 40ft in diameter. In the 1920s the fountain's majolica facing began to crack and the statue of St George and the Dragon, which had been located on the top of the fountain, had fallen down. The borough council took the fountain away in 1926. In 1927, when widening of Cambridge Heath Road was undertaken, a section of land was removed from the museum grounds and a bronze statue, the 'Eagle Slayer' designed by John Bell in 1847, was erected in the grounds. It was moved to the rear of the grounds at one point but returned in January 1961.

Hamilton Road, June 1953. A street party, presumably to celebrate the Queen's Coronation. The children seem to be enjoying their day and the food on offer. One boy in fact seems to be so distracted by the food on offer he is ignoring the camera, unlike everyone else visible in this picture.

The mayor of Bethnal Green (Councillor G.R.H. Hemsley, JP) speaks to children on the steps of Bethnal Green Town Hall before they leave for a day out to Clacton-on-Sea, 13 July 1948. Around 204 children went on this trip in eight coaches, although some of the children in this picture look somewhat apprehensive about what lies ahead. At Clacton they had a three-course lunch with ice cream and, after a day's entertainment, on their return to Bethnal Green Town Hall they were each given a toy, an apple and a souvenir card of the outing. Ten members of this Guild of nineteen businessmen, some of whom had been connected with a lubricating engine oil company, accompanied the children along with the mayor and mayoress and eight nurses from Bethnal Green Hospital.

Trip to the zoo, 10 July 1952. Youngsters and parents about to embark on a trip to Chessington Zoo from Collingwood Estate, Cambridge Heath Road. This trip was organized by Collingwood Estate Tenant's Association. One can see by looking at their faces how excited the children are.

Boarding coaches outside Bethnal Green Town Hall, June 1949. This outing to Southend-on-Sea was organized by the Bethnal Green Old People's Welfare Committee, first established in 1948, and proved very popular. Over 200 old age pensioners made the trip in eight coaches. Mr Percy Holman, MP for Bethnal Green, can be seen in the centre of the photograph.

Coronation Day, Jesus Hospital Estate, June 1953. Coronation Day in Bethnal Green saw many forms of celebration take place; street parties as illustrated here were common. Public dancing took place in Bethnal Green Gardens from 8 p.m.-11 p.m. and was floodlit. This was after displays and activities by various local organizations taking place between 6.30 p.m. and 8 p.m. The council provided coronation gifts to many in the borough and the officers and men of HMS *Crane*, the borough's adopted warship, each received a pint glass tankard inscribed with the borough's badge.

Bethnal Green old folk going on an outing, June 1951. The mayor of Bethnal Green performs the official send-off to Bethnal Green's pensioners as they embark on a trip to Margate organized by the Old People's Welfare Committee. Councillor H.E. Tate, chairman of the Old People's Welfare Committee, is in the centre of this picture wearing a beret. Ten coaches took 300 members of the Committee, which by this time had five clubs. These clubs would organize outings and trips to shows. The mayor and mayoress of Margate took lunch with the members during their visit to Margate.

Two views of Angela Burdett-Coutts Fountain, Victoria Park, an illustration from 1862 and a photograph taken in 1970. Although only seventy acres of Victoria Park's 217 acres lie within the boundaries of Bethnal Green, it plays an important role in the social life of the inhabitants of the area and so deserves inclusion in this book. This fountain was built to provide clean drinking water to the local populace. H.A. Darbishire designed it in an Italian Gothic Style and it was built with Sicilian marble, Cornish granite and Caen Limestone. When this fountain was built in 1862, clean drinking water was seen by many as a vital element of preserving good health and stopping diseases such as cholera. The fountain still serves today, not as a drinking fountain but as an impressive focal point in the park.

Members of the Band of Vocal Sacred Music, Victoria Park, stand outside the Burdett-Coutts Fountain, 1865. This meeting took place on the north side of the fountain on Sunday evenings. These meetings started on 11 June 1865. This may be the earliest surviving photograph of Victoria Park.

Victoria Park, a drinking fountain being used by children, *c.* 1909. The park, named after Queen Victoria, was built to help improve the health of the overcrowded local inhabitants by giving them breathing space. Laid out by James Pennethorne, it was opened in 1845 although it was in unofficial use by 1843. Former brick fields, which were valued for their rich beds of clay, were converted into lakes. Some of the parkland was once Bonner Fields, a place where religious opponents in the days of Bishop Bonner in the fifteenth century would be put to death by burning. The park has, in its time, played its part in the history of national campaign movements, ranging from the Chartist demonstrations which saw Royal Horse Guards deployed to the park in June 1848, through to open-air meetings conducted by Eleanor Marx and at other times Sylvia Pankhurst's suffragettes. It was in Victoria Park that Oswald Mosely addressed 5,000 fascist followers in July 1936. This meeting was followed by rioting and paved the way for what was to come in October 1936, the 'Battle of Cable Street'. The park also hosted, on a somewhat more tasteful occasion, the Sadler's Wells Ballet performance during one week in August 1942. John Bright (1811-1889), to whom the fountain is dedicated, was a radical politician. He entered parliament in 1843 and fought on many issues, attacking aristocracy, privilege, and the removal of the civil and political restrictions that were imposed on British Jews. He also wished for an extension of the franchise. Presumably, however, the dedication is in memory of his support of the temperance movement. The drinking fountain may have been deliberately placed here to offer a different type of beverage to the one found in the public house in the background, the Morpeth Castle.

Victoria Park, people sitting near the pagoda, August 1913. The Chinese Pagoda originally formed the entrance to a Chinese exhibition in Knightsbridge in 1847. It was bought for £110 from the Chinese Collection at Hyde Park. The Pagoda was demolished in 1956 due to war damage and general wear and tear.

Boating Lake, Victoria Park, photographed from the Lake Bridge, c. 1930. Like the people in the photograph, the author has used this lake in the past for leisure pursuits, and many hours were spent waiting to catch the big fish!

Boating Lake, Victoria Park, 1900. Children feed the waterfowl; an activity that continues to this day. 'Vicky Park', as it is known by locals, has always proved popular with families. During the Whitsun holiday on 6 June 1892, 300,000 people visited the park. It continues to serve today as a place of relaxation for the local population.